YOUR KNOWLEDGE HAS VALUE

Opportunities and limits of an internal IT with a multi-project management approach

Matthias Herreiner

Bibliographic information published by the German National Library:

The German National Library lists this publication in the National Bibliography; detailed bibliographic data are available on the Internet at http://dnb.dnb.de.

ISBN: 9783346864482
This book is also available as an ebook.

© GRIN Publishing GmbH
Trappentreustraße 1
80339 München

Print and binding: Books on Demand GmbH, Norderstedt, Germany
Printed on acid-free paper from responsible sources.

The present work has been carefully prepared. Nevertheless, authors and publishers do not incur liability for the correctness of information, notes, links and advice as well as any printing errors.

GRIN web shop: https://www.grin.com/document/1348063

Hochschule für angewandte Wissenschaften
-Fachhochschule Deggendorf-
Fakultät Betriebswirtschaft und Wirtschaftsinformatik
(Master-Studiengang Wirtschaftsinformatik)

Opportunities and limits of an internal IT
with a multi-project management approach

Term paper curriculum International Project Management

Vorgelegt von:
Matthias Herreiner
am: 15.01.2011

Contents

List of Figures

1 Introduction

In the seventies electronic data processing was a big issue for several companies. Early systems were big number crunchers and were installed exclusively by large organizations. Nowadays the situation has changed. Data processing departments were renamed to IT departments and the IT is available to the smallest company. In the last years a lot of the internal IT departments were outsourced to reduce the costs. But later it was recognized that it is not always the best way to compete with others particularly in terms of the globalization without an own IT. Those companies which kept their IT department also have problems. The IT is often considered as a black box with own rules. Projects which need IT resources move often into a dependency on the IT.

In the last years the number of projects increased enormously. The high number of projects ends in a high requirement for the IT department. The problem ist that nearly every project needs IT resources. Another problem is that in most companies several projects are handled simultaneously. For that the IT must be efficiently organized with standardized processes to meet the demand for the resources. The classic project management has no tool in the portfolio to manage simultaneous projects and the resources because only a single project is considered. A new approach is needed which is the missing link between the classic project management and the handling of simultaneous projects. An efficient way to handle several projects at the same time is the multi-project management (MPM) approach which could close the gap.

In this abstract the role of an internal IT and the handling of IT projects is discussed. The success factors of a good project and the problems which can occur are inspected. Furthermore an MPM approach for the handling of several simultaneous projects is shown.

2 The role of an internal IT department

Nowadays companies are moving from the industrialized society to the information society [RSGN10]. Information has a new dimension of quantity and quality. Never before it was so easy to get information and to make profit with it. So it is necessary that companies have a competent partner who provides information and relevant data to support the own business processes. In some cases companies decided to run internal IT departments and no external service provider.

In the Seventies companies started to invest in IT technology and set up the first data processing departments to automate their processes. The result was that manual based activities could be handled in a better way for e.g. the prompt printing of invoices and the faster handling of the incoming payments. In the Eighties the PC and integrated systems like SAP started their triumphal procession. They helped the companies to optimize their business processes. In the Nineties ERP systems stepped in the game. The benefit was that with these ERP systems different business processes could be integrated and optimized over several value-added steps. As a result costs and redundant interfaces could be reduced.

Although in many companies the IT departments and their infrastructure helps the company to compete with others the costs were often mentioned. But costs are not the only factor to measure the value of the IT. With the upcoming of the internet and the world-wide-web a change was made. It is more important to realize the value potential of an internal IT department than just thinking about the cost factor. With an effective and forceful IT department it is easier to enter a foreign market and to deal with the globalization. But not in all companies the necessary change was realized. The common view of the IT is just a service provider which has to act on demand. But the IT should be a part of a pro-active approach to identify the potentials in the company.

In comparison with competitors the IT could be used as a strategic weapon. For this it is necessary to setup an IT strategy and a CIO who is responsible for the development of the IT strategy. The CIO has to deal with the CEO so that is possible to design and architecture the company together. Innovative projects could be detected and the ability to compete with others could be increased.

A survey of A.T. Kearney in Growth Excellence 2006 revealed that IT is in the top five of growth barriers for companies. Main problems of internal IT departments are [ERS08, S. 59]:

- Data inconsistency and data redundancy. Often a piece was added without considering the whole thing.

- The involvement of the IT was too late in the decision and design process of projects.

- Less Transparency of the IT Department. It is often considered as a black box with inefficient interfaces.

To solve these problems it is nowadays important to join the IT strategy with the company strategy. The IT department doesn't have to wait for incoming requests but rather look for innovative projects. The company has to answer the question: How should we organize our company, especially the managing of projects with the IT, to handle efficiently the world and the problems of tomorrow.

2.1 The need of project management

In companies the daily business is changing. It becomes more and more project-driven than task-driven. The reason for that is the increasing complexity of the requirements. More and more stakeholders are involved and a lot of dependencies are to handle. Nowadays nearly every change in a company results in an IT project. New law regulations, changes of the business processes or the organizational structures have to be adopted in the IT systems. The globalization and the resulting global competition increases also the pressure for the companies. The IT has become a key role. It is more and more important to have an effective IT because the interval of the projects and the demand for IT resources has increased. Often it will be realized that there is a strong dependency on the IT. For this reason it is very important to involve the IT at an early stage. In order to handle the projects and to reduce the project-cycle time it is necessary to setup an efficient and professional project management.

The Definition of the Project Management Institute (PMI) for Project Management is [PMI08]: "Project Management is the application of knowledge, skills, tools and techniques to project activities to meet project requirements". In many inhouse IT departments project management is implemented separately. That means that the IT department has an own process model to handle the demanding projects. The V-Modell-XT is such a process model which could be chosen from the IT for the managing of IT projects.

The V-model-XT is the successor of the V-model 97 and is a extreme tailored version of the V-model 97 [VMODXT]. It has the benefit that the model can be customized for individual needs and requirements. The model defines a series of documents which are called products. The products are the final results of different project steps. In Figure 2.1 the main steps of the systems development cycle is shown.

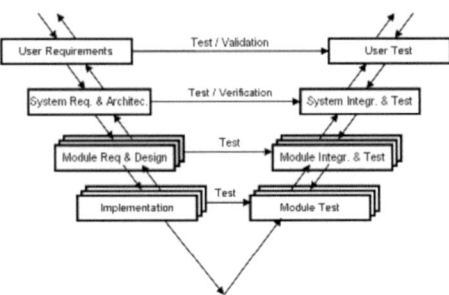

Figure 2.1: V-model of the systems engineering process

The graphical representation of the steps are V-shaped. That is the reason for the name V-model. The model is similar to the classic waterfall model as it is quite rigid and contains many iterations. One product of the V-model is the requirement specification. The specification mainly consists of:

- User Requirement Specifications

- Functional Requirement Specifications

- Design Specifications

The specifications are often created by the departments of a company. After finishing the requirement specifications they will be sent to the IT. The IT checks if the requirements are formally complete. If the specification is complete it will be formulated in a more detailed functional specification. After that a project will be launched in a kick-off meeting and a project manager is selected.

In the next step a software architect takes the functional specification and builds a software architecture. This product consists of the main components of the software to be built. The software architecture is a rough draft and is specified in more detail in the next step.

The result of the next design step is the product software specification. The software specification is the working basis for the software developer. It should be as detailed as possible so that the developer can start the programming quickly and effectively. After finishing a part of the software the testing of the module starts. In the testing phase the requesting department and the IT must be involved. Usually a separated testing area is used to bring the software in a productive state. If any errors will be detected the errors will be fixed in the next iteration of the software development cycle. So the software quality will increase in each iteration.

The benefit of a standardized process model is that the project-cycle time could be reduced and the quality of the project results increases. Besides these advantages there are often some problems in practice. Main concepts of a process model are more theoretically based. Problems in managing projects with a process model are not unusual.

2.2 Problems of managing Projects

Managing projects is often a big challenge. A lot of stakeholders are to satisfy and the project leader has to deal with several problems. Additionally the project should be finished in time and money. Especially the managing of projects with an IT aspect and the involvement of an internal IT Department is quite a challenge. A good IT project depends on several success factors:

- *Qualified project manager:* For the success of a project it is important that a good project manager is selected at the start of the project. The project stands or falls with a good project manager. A good manager needs a lot of experience and only the best employees should be considered to be a project manager. For the support and the qualifying of the project manager trainings should be started. Often the role of a project manager is not absolutely clear. A clear role definition is necessary because the responsibility and the authority has to be defined exactly. The project manager has to know about his tasks and duties. Without a clear definition everybody relies on the other. Another problem is that in many companies with an internal IT department there are several project managers at the same time. The first project manager is provided by the requesting department the second by the IT department. This situation has a lot of conflict potential. A possible solution could be that one project manager is the senior manager and the other project manager is subordinated to avoid turf wars.

- *Conflict between line- and project organization:* Moreover there is often a conflict between the line and the project organization. The line manager has the fear that he loses influence and that he is no longer at the forefront of progress. In many cases the line manager has the opinion that he is the man who makes the decisions. Additionally he has the fears that the best employees will be grabbed by the project manager. So it is absolutely necessary that the line and the project manager have a clear area of responsibility. This is an important factor for the success of a project. Many companies with an internal IT department are especially affected by this problem. The IT department manager doesn't want to share his resources with others and the IT should remain as his weapon. So it is necessary that the project manager has appropriate soft skills especially argumentation and communication strength to represent the project. Finally it is important that the line organization is subordinated to the project organization.

- *Support from the Management:* Additionally it is very important that the project and the project manager have the support from the management. The executive officers have to support and to push the project. The corporate culture must be project friendly and in the kick-off the project charter must be communicated from the top-management so that it is clear for everybody. Through the support friction loss could be avoided and the resources won't be wasted. The supporting of the top management is one of the biggest success factors.

- *No Standards for project management:* A weak point of companies with internal IT departments is that there are no standards for the project management. Each department implements their own project management in a special way. The IT has it's own process model and mostly the rest of the company has a different process model. A lot of redundancy and friction loss between the IT and the departments is the result. However the special requirements and the special needs of the IT must be considered. The special position of the IT is nowadays and in the future unavoidable. One reason for that is that the whole technical aspect in the projects could often only considered and inspected by the IT. For this reason a house-wide standardized project management is absolutely necessary. It declares standards for the whole company and is mandatory for everybody. The benefit is that projects could be finished earlier and the quality of the results is increasing.

- *Portfolio of software tools:* Another point for the success of the project manager and finally the project is a portfolio of software tools which supports the whole project process and the main steps. Effective tools play a key role. They should be able to generate reports with detailed information for the stakeholders and provide effective methods to support the project manager in the planning phase. An important function which is necessary in the tool portfolio is the planning and management of resources.

Besides the indicated success factors and problems the number of projects have been increased in the last years. The problem is that the classic project management is optimized for the managing of one single project. In companies normally severals projects are handled simultaneously. The dependencies on other projects are not really considered. So every project manager fights for his project. Especially between IT projects there is often a strong correlation. In most cases IT projects are changing a system environment or are adding new components. Different results of the projects have to be reintegrated in the system environment. In these integration process a lot of conflicts could appear if the projects are not considered and matched together during the whole project phase. One opportunity to handle several projects at the same time is to set up an efficient multi-project management.

3 Multi-project-management the missing link

As indicated there is often a strong correlation between simultaneous projects especially with IT aspects. If several projects are in a substantive relationship an overview is needed. The multi-project management (MPM) approach deals with the relationship of strategic decisions and several simultaneous projects. The strategic component of MPM is the prioritize of possible projects with a high strategic value for the company. The operative component of MPM is to find out and control the dependencies between the projects. Main points of the MPM approach are:

- The forward-looking of resource conflicts.

- Avoid and inspect conflicting objectives between different projects.

- The use of synergies and avoidance of redundancy and recognition of substantive dependencies.

In order to manage the main points of MPM there is a new role, the multi-project manager (MPM manager) necessary. The multi-project manager has no direct project responsibility. It is an internal consultant for the project managers, the management board and the department managers. The tasks of the MPM manager is broader. He has to keep all ongoing projects in view. For that he has to analyze the projects more in the broad than in depth. To keep the projects in view, it is necessary to have a standardized project management so that the projects are handled in the same way. Especially the parameter time, costs, resources and contents of a project are very important for the MPM manager. This parameters have to be inspected for dependencies by the MPM manager. One challenge of simultaneous projects is that some resources must be shared. For e.g. a software developer which has a special skill or an IT architect with detailed process know how. In addition to the limited availability of the resources there is often a big problem with the scheduling of the IT resources. Besides the working in the project they have to ensure their daily business. So there is a big conflict potential between the project tasks and the daily business. Usually this ends with a dispute between the project manager and the line manager. For that the MPM manager has to schedule the resources for the project tasks and the line business. This is not an easy job and the MPM manager needs the support of a software program which helps to solve the problem. At first the software has to input all resources (e.g. developers) with their skills. In the next step the software needs information about all the projects with their priority and their needs. Now the available resources are allocated to the request with the highest priority. This is a classical optimization problem which has to be solved by the software. After finishing the scheduling of resources the MPM manager needs the opportunity to intervene manually.

Besides the scheduling the main task of the MPM manager is to identify conflicting objectives between different projects and the prioritization of the projects.

3.1 Prioritization of projects

The prioritization of projects in MPM is an ongoing process. All ongoing and new projects are included in the prioritization. Some projects will be rejected in reason of a k.o. criteria. Other projects are high pressure projects which means that they have to be launched immediately. For all the projects a capital value and a strategic value has to be determined. With these two values the projects could be classified and displayed in a portfolio diagram. In Figure 3.1 four classes are displayed in which a project can be classified [TM10, S. 7].

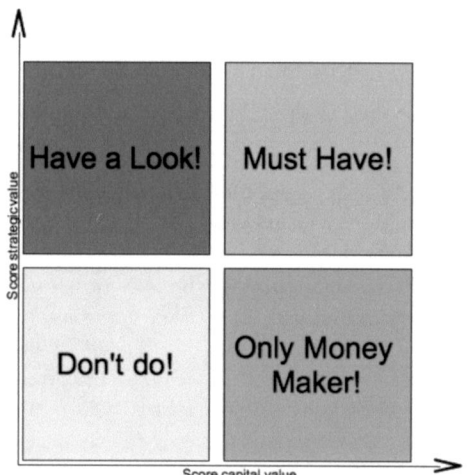

Figure 3.1: Portfolio diagram for project prioritization

Projects which are located in the square "Have a Look!" are projects with a high strategic value, less complexity and a low capital value for the company. Projects in this square are in the long term useful but the launch must be checked exactly. The square "Only Money Maker!" represents projects with a low strategic value with high complexity and a high capital value for the company. That means that the total use of the project has to be checked. The project prioritization helps the MPM manager and the management to get a ranking and a simple overview of all the projects. After the prioritizing of the projects the relevant projects could be launched or stopped. After finding and launching the right projects for the company it is necessary to identify the conflicting objectives between the different projects.

3.2 Analysis of project dependencies

The identification of dependencies between several projects is a difficult part. The MPM manager needs an instrument to check the projects. The classic project management doesn't have a suitable method in the portfolio. A simple instrument is the interdependence analysis which is an easy and effective method. The interdependence analysis helps the MPM manager to check the projects for synergies and conflicts. The results of the analysis could be used to give the project managers some recommendations and hints for their projects. Basis oft the interdependence analysis is a simple matrix with all the projects in the rows and columns. For each project combination a score value has to be determined. In Figure 3.2 an exemplary matrix for the analyzing of project dependencies is illustrated [TM10, S. 8].

Dependency 0 = small 3 = medium 6 = strong	Relaunch Online-Shop	SAP Launch	CRM-Functionality Add On	Market Entry Italy	Release Change Database	Total Push
	1	2	3	4	5	
1 Relaunch Online-Shop		3	3	6	3	15
2 SAP Launch	3		6	6	6	21
3 CRM-Functionality Add On	3	0		3	0	6
4 Market Entry Italy	3	3	3		0	9
5 Release Change Database	3	0	0	3		6
Total Pull	13	8	15	22	14	

Figure 3.2: Interdependence matrix to analyze dependencies of projects

For the creating and filling the matrix the following steps are necessary [TM10, S. 7f.]:

1. *All projects have to be considered*

2. *Creating a Matrix of all projects in rows and columns*

3. *Rating of all project combinations in the matrix.* In this step each project is compared with each other. For every combination it has to be checked if another project is influenced. The strength of the influence could be rated in several steps. For e.g. 0 - no influence; 3 - medium influence; 6 - strong influence.

4. *Determination of the row total.* The row total is an index which represents the push factor of a project. It describes the influence of a single project on all the other projects. The higher the index is the more the other projects are influenced.

5. *Determination of the column total.* The column total is a index which represents the pull factor of a project. It describes the influence of all the other projects to a single project. The higher the index is the more the project is influenced by the others.

6. *Display the projects in a portfolio dependency diagram.*

The project "SAP Launch" in Figure 3.2 represents a strong push project because it has a high push score and a low pull score. This project has to be kept in view all the time. The project "Relaunch Online Shop" is scored with nearly the same push and pull score. That means that the relaunch of the online shop influences other projects. At the same time the project is influenced by several other projects. For this project it is very important to ensure the communication between the different project managers.

In the last step the scored projects can be displayed in a portfolio diagram. The diagram is similar to Figure 3.1 but with a different meaning. It should helps the MPM manager to give the project managers recommendations and to get an overview of the criticality of the projects. Through the portfolio diagram the projects can be classified in four criticality classes [TM10, S. 9]:

- *Critical projects*
  Critical projects are influencing several other projects and at the same time they are influenced by several others. These projects are difficult to handle and the complexity is larger than others. The projects have to be kept in view all the time and the project managers have to be updated regularly. The early detection of problems is very important for those projects.

- *Push (active) projects*
  Push projects have a strong influence on other projects. The project manager has to communicate changes and problems as soon as possible to the other project managers. Push projects are not really affected by other projects.

- *Pull (passive) projects*
  Pull projects have a small influence on other projects. The project managers have to ensure that they are updated in regular intervals by the relevant project managers. Pull projects are not really affecting other projects.

- *Non critical projects*
  Non critical projects have a small influence on other projects and are hardly influenced by others. So the managing of these projects is not critical and they are detached from the others.

3.3 Successful multi-project management

The success factors of MPM are similar to the classic project management factors (section 2.2). But MPM is not a panacea. It is a meta layer which extends the classic project management. It is necessary for companies with several ongoing simultanueos projects. MPM provides a set of tools to get a simple overview about all projects. The support of software tools in MPM is much more important than in the classic project management (e.g. dependency analysis, prioritization and resource planning). The tools play a key role in this way. For companies with an internal IT department it is important that the prioritization of the projects are handled outside of the IT. This guarantees that the right projects with an high strategic value ("Must Haves!") are forced. A further benefit is that the IT has less effort with the whole MPM process so they can focus their skills on their core competence. However, the IT respectively the CIO could consult the MPM manager and the management board when the projects are scored. Moreover an embedding of MPM in the organizational structure of a company is absolutely necessary. The MPM must be a part of the whole culture in the company. For this point the management is the relevant part. The support from the management board is as important as the competence of the MPM manager role. A MPM manager who is not equipped with appropriate rights has no chance and the MPM is doomed to fail. Finally in MPM the whole communication process is much more important than in the classic project management.

The core of the success of MPM is similar to the classic project management. It's the simple project member for e.g. a developer. A powerful and experienced project team is often more valuable than the correct process model to have. The project manager has to look for the right team and the motivation of them. In MPM there is the danger that the model becomes unpopular because the team could think that MPM is only a new buzzword and the end of the story is often more bureaucracy than effects. So the MPM manager and the project manager should together explain the MPM approach and the benefit of it to the team.

4 Conclusion

Companies are moving from the industrialized society to the information society. It is more and more important to have an strategic weapon who provides the relevant information efficiently. One opportunity is to run an own IT department. On one hand they were often considered as a black box, but on the other hand they are a powerful strategic weapon which helps efficiently to deal with the globalization and the entry into foreign markets. Besides the advantages of an own IT there are also some problems in handling IT projects. One problem is that the project-cycle time is too long. To reduce the problems it is necessary to setup an standardized process model. But a process model alone is not enough for a good project.

In practice a good IT project depends on several success factors. For each project role there is a clear area of responsibility and a clear communication to the whole project team necessary. A clear communication and responsibility could reduce the conflict potential between the team the project manager and the line manager. Another important success factor is the support from the management and the integration of the project culture in the whole company culture so that it's clear for everybody. But the most important success factor is the project manager and the project team. A good project manager and a motivated team is often more valuable then the right process model to have.

Due to the increasing number of projects and the access to the same resources it is necessary to integrate a multi-project management approach to handle simultaneous projects. The benefit of an MPM approach is the identification of resource conflicts and conflicting objectives between different projects. To provide this benefit it's necessary to setup a new role the MPM manager. The MPM manager is an internal consultant for the project managers and the management and ensures the communication between the project managers. The MPM approach provides a prioritization of projects which helps the company to find out the right projects with a high strategic value. For each project a score value is determined which represents the ranking of a project. The score value helps the MPM manager to create a portfolio diagram to determine the right projects. Another useful tool in the MPM process is the interdependence matrix to analyze the dependencies of the projects. For a good MPM approach the success factors are related to the classic project management. But in MPM the whole communication is much more important. Furthermore an effective software portfolio is indispensable to support the MPM manager and the project managers in each project phase. The software portfolio should provide detailed information about the projects and should help the managers in the resource planning phase.

Finally MPM is a good approach for a modern IT to cope with everyday life - but is not a panacea. It is important to avoid too much bureaucracy and to communicate the objectives with the support of the top management. But sometimes it is enough to have a simple and motivated project team with a mixture of new and experienced members for a good project.

Bibliography

[ERS08] EUL, Marcus ; RÖDER, Holger ; SIMONS, Edgar: *Strategisches IT-Management: vom Kostenfaktor zum Werttreiber.* 2008

[PMI08] *A guide to the project management body of knowledge: (PMBOK® guide).* 4. Ausg. Newtown Square, Pa. : PMI, 2008 (PMI global standard)

[RSGN10] RÜTER, Andreas ; SCHRÖDER, Jürgen ; GÖLDNER, Axel ; NIEBUHR, Jens: *IT-Governance in der Praxis: Erfolgreiche Positionierung der IT im Unternehmen. Anleitung zur erfolgreichen Umsetzung regulatorischer und wettbewerbsbedingter Anforderungen.* Berlin, Heidelberg : Springer-Verlag Berlin Heidelberg, 2010 (Xpert.press)

[TM10] MÜLLER, Arno ; VON THIENEN, Lars: *Einsatz des Multi-Projekt-Management zur Optimierung des IT-Controlling.* www.bps.de/files/bps-beitrag-projektmgt-mpm.pdf, Abruf: 28.12.2010

[VMODXT] *V-Modell XT.* http://v-modell.iabg.de/v-modell-xt-html/index.html, Abruf: 28.12.2010